CW01064349

A BRIDGE BETWEEN THE SPIRITUAL AND NATURAL REALMS

A BRIDGE BETWEEN THE
SPIRITUAL AND
NATURAL REALMS

Nicole Zilinskas

PALMETTO
PUBLISHING
Charleston, SC
www.PalmettoPublishing.com

Hardcover ISBN: 979-8-8229-4284-4
Paperback ISBN: 979-8-8229-4285-1
eBook ISBN: 979-8-8229-4286-8

TABLE OF CONTENTS

PROLOGUE

My people are destroyed for lack of knowledge.

—Hosea 4:6

If you have opened this book, then God is inviting you to grow in knowledge and relationship with Him.

He wants to encourage you to draw on his love and word regardless of any turmoil in your life or the world because the truth will always set you free.

If you cannot find a natural solution to a spiritual problem, learn to rest in God's word and knowledge; he has the ability to make things happen.

The enemy cannot move in an atmosphere of love. Christians, this is where we hold our core power. When the enemy feeds on fear and hate, speak love over anyone who has wrongly accused you. This paralyzes their actions and holds their Tongue to silence, sending confusion into the enemy's camp.

Radiate love over your family and friends, and then watch how God will move heaven and earth to bring peace and reconciliation.

Victory in His Name.

PREFACE

My sheep hear my voice, I know them,
and they follow me.

—JOHN 10:27

To God, be the glory of everything in my life.

This book is about my spiritual journey and walk with the Holy Spirit. You will read about one person's obedience to God's calling. I consider it such an honor and privilege to be invited to participate in the end time's warfare.

As you come along on a journey with me and experience profound and exciting adventures with our Lord, imagine what God could move in your life if you would hear His Voice and follow Him.

INTRODUCTION

HOW THE LORD TRAINED ME UP ONE-ON-ONE FOR SPIRITUAL WARFARE

The Holy Spirit spent eight months training me for spiritual warfare in my home, before giving me my first assignment.

Through a series of everyday events, I found myself invited to a long weekend conference through a church I was attending at the time. Two friends were excited to go and had asked me to come with them; I eagerly accepted.

I wasn't quite sure what to expect, thinking it was maybe a Bible study class of some kind to help me grow in the Lord. I found out that this was a training school called the "Ministry of Spiritual Gifts," similar to the Bill Hamon prophetic training with Christian International.

When we arrived, each person was given a training manual and instructed to sit and wait in a room for a prophetic word to be spoken to them. When my name was called, I was greeted by a man, who was a seasoned prophet, and a female trainee. The trainee watched as the man took my hands, started speaking in tongues, and prayed over me. When he opened his eyes, I noticed his energy was filled with love from the Holy Spirit; he was eager to share my destiny with me.

He called me a mighty warrior in the end times and said that I would be used in the healing and deliverance ministry for God's kingdom to touch and heal hundreds of lives. This sounded very foreign to me as I had never heard authority spoken with such confidence; the man explained that I would personally be trained by the Holy Spirit in my home. Again, I thought it was an odd thing to say, as my limited experience and knowledge of such things in the church or outside had never prepared me for such a destiny.

The trainee also spoke over me with precise accuracy; three years later, after twice a year of training, I would be a graduate of the Ministry of Spiritual Gifts training school and have the opportunity to speak with a teaching prophet and prophesier over a new student speaking their God-given gifts.

***

A word spoken over me.

—Isaiah 42

There is much work to be done, and you will touch hundreds of lives. Keep praying and worshipping more; you will come under attack because of your work for the Lord.

You are an anointed seer, a trailblazer. Someone who paves a new and different path, and people will want to be near you because you have the courage to do things in a different way. Because of your obedience, I will give you the desires of your heart.

Through a series of events, my prophetic destiny that the man had spoken about happened, and I jumped into training with the Holy Spirit guiding, protecting, and encouraging me. I had no one to turn to for what was about to take place, only to trust the prophetic word and hold on tight for the one-on-one training.

This is how it began.

***

My mother-in-law was very ill and came to live with us for four months before she passed away and went home to the Lord.

About three weeks after the funeral, I had a dream that I was looking out of my bedroom window at the lake where we live. It was dark, and I noticed our bench, which looks out over the water, had a giant being sitting there. I could only see the back of this entity; it wore a long robe with a hood. As I continued to stare, the demon knew I was watching; it slightly turned its head toward my window. I could not see its face, but fear paralyzed me; the demon spoke in my head and said it was waiting for an appointed time to enter my house. I woke up from the dream and lay there in my bed afraid of what I had seen.

My once peaceful and happy home had now turned into my training ground for encounters with the supernatural. A few weeks went by and all was quiet, then one night while I was sleeping, I woke up to a sound in my bedroom. It sounded like a smacking noise, kind of like when someone smacks their lips while eating. As my eyes adjusted to the darkness of the room, I saw two evil red eyes hovering over me and a winged creature smacking its lips and staring at me. This reminded me of those gargoyles that you would see on medieval castles. I lay there frozen and paralyzed in fear, not knowing what to do; I couldn't even speak or call out to my husband, who was sleeping peacefully next to me.

Then, like a ray of sunshine, a voice spoke into my head: "Pray". As soon as I had my first orders from the Holy Spirit, I started calling out my love for Jesus, and the demon recoiled, lifted slowly off my bed, and flew out the window.

Over many months of different scenarios, I became familiar with hearing the Lord's voice. He would take me into dreams for my training, and when I was afraid of something that tried to attack me, the Holy Spirit would teach me to counter the attack by speaking love over the enemy. He showed me that the enemy cannot move or harm you in an atmosphere of love and to always walk in peace. He told me that I would always be protected.

As I grew stronger in the spiritual realm, I noticed I was on my own sometimes and was surprised that my strong warrior spirit stood its ground with the enemy, speaking in my spirit language.

Then I started having dreams of places where I would eventually do deliverances for people. I knew the homes, locations, and people I was to meet and help. I kept a journal of my dreams and experiences with the Holy Spirit; I have a nickname for Him: "Holy friend." He has kindly corrected and disciplined me along the way when I would jump ahead of my decision making. He truly is a wonderful trainer and helper here on Earth.

Jesus said to His disciples before he died that He would send a helper, the Holy Spirit.

John 15:26: I will send you the Helper from the Father. The helper is the Spirit of Truth, who comes from the Father. When he comes, he will tell about me.

CHAPTER 1
THE GIRL AT STARBUCKS

MY FIRST ASSIGNMENT

*Trust in the Lord with all your heart and lean not
into your own understanding; in all your ways ac-
knowledge him, and he will make your paths straight.*

—PROVERBS 3:5–6

I had arranged to meet a Christian friend for a cup of coffee at
Starbucks, and as we ordered our coffee, I noticed the server
behind the counter. She was a beautiful young woman with long
black hair and pretty brown eyes, with a lovely smile. I was in-
stantly drawn to her neck, which had a very large goiter there; it
distracted you from her beauty. As I paid for my drink, I heard
the Holy Spirit say, "Heal her." My natural mind was thinking,
"I'm here to chat with a friend over coffee, and there is a line of
people waiting to place their orders, so how can I heal her with
so much happening around me?" I took my coffee and headed
over to the table where my friend was waiting. I asked her if she
wouldn't mind waiting a little while because the Holy Spirit had
told me to heal the women behind the counter. I looked back

1

at the young woman, and nobody was in line, so I went up and approached her. I asked if she was a Christian, and she excitedly said yes. I said I was too. I asked her about the goiter on her throat, and she told me that she had always had it and that it would not get any larger. Her doctor said there was nothing to be done about it.

I mentioned to her that the Lord uses me in the healing and deliverance ministry and that I was told to heal her; she became very excited and asked, "Where do you want to do the healing?" God had already prepared her heart to receive her anointing. I looked around and didn't see anywhere private, so I asked her for a suggestion. She replied that the bathroom would be the only place. I was amused as it was a single bathroom, and two women going in there together must have looked strange, especially as we locked the door behind us. I pulled out my anointing oil from the purse I was carrying and asked her to reconfirm with me her love for Jesus and to say the sinner's prayer.

We both prayed together. I do this at the beginning of all healings and deliverances so that we stand as a clean slate before the Lord when I'm preparing to speak over people. I anointed her forehead with the sign of the cross and poured some oil in the palm of my hand, then laid my hand over the goiter. I started praying in the Spirit, and energy and heat flowed through my body and hands. I commanded in the name of Jesus Christ to bind, pull out from the root, and send this curse where Jesus would send it. The young woman was filled with hope for her healing and was happy to receive a blessing from our Lord. We hugged, and I explained that I would be keeping her in my prayers for forty days and reading Psalm 91 as a hedge of protection around her, and she was to do the same.

Afterward, I went back to sit and chat with my friend, enjoying my coffee while the woman at the counter continued on with her work.

The forty days had finished, and a couple of months went by. I often thought of the beautiful women that I had laid hands on to receive her healing and wondered how she was. During those days of prayer, I would sometimes hear the enemy enter my head and tell me not to stop by the coffee shop because she still had a huge lump on her throat. I pushed the thought aside and claimed her full health. Another couple of months went by, and a friend's birthday was coming up, so I decided to stop at Starbucks to pick up a gift card.

As I entered, there was the usual line to the counter, so I waited quietly for my turn to order. I actually didn't expect to see the young woman again, but lo and behold, there she was taking people's orders. When it was my turn, she asked, "How can I help you?" When I spoke, she recognized my voice and called my name, and I smiled at her. She ran her hand down her throat where the goiter had once been and told me it's smooth and gone; it left that night. We both hugged each other and had tears of joy at the supernatural healing and blessing she had received.

Several months went by, and my daughter and I were heading out to check on her horse; we decided to drive through Starbucks for some hot coffee and a pastry. As I went to place my order, a friendly, familiar face looked down into my car. She called my name and said, "What's going on in God's world?"

Over many years with assignments from the Lord, I have enjoyed my training and our close time together. Jesus, truly, is our best friend and always protects and looks after His people here during their journey on Earth.

CHAPTER 2

THE WITCH AT THE HEALTH FOOD STORE

MATTHEW 18:18

One day I went to a health food store to pick up some supplements. It was a favorite place of mine to go, and the staff there were extremely knowledgeable. They had a unique way of pairing vitamins and supplements to fit your lifestyle and any changes that were needed along the way.

On this particular day, only one person was there working. I was the only one in the store besides a lady behind the cash register.

She politely asked if I needed any help, and we started up a conversation. The lady informed me that she was the manager of the store in the next town and was just helping out that day.

She had a keen interest in people's needs and told me that she quite often made gift baskets for anyone who had lost a family member or was ill. The kindness of her heart made me smile and want to know more about her, especially as I had once been a volunteer for hospice and spent many hours sitting with dying patients, comforting them and their families.

We talked about aromatherapy oils, such as lavender, which has a soothing and calming effect on the body, as well as chamomile herbal teas. I made a mental note of her gift basket idea for future hospice families.

The woman then proceeded to tell me that she "clears houses" from unwanted spirits and that she was a psychic. I told her that I was a seer in God's world, and then I explained that in heaven, her God-given gift was a seer, but she was using it in a worldly way. I told her that when she saw spirits, they were called unfamiliar spirits, were demonic in nature, and were witchcraft. She was fascinated by how the Lord used me and said we have a lot in common and that she loved to talk about the supernatural.

I agreed, but explained in a kind and loving way that I was a seer in the Lord's army, and everything I did was according to God's will through fasting, praying, and confirmations for others.

Her spirit was so moved at that moment that she asked to pray with me; she asked the Lord to forgive her sins; and I spoke the deliverance prayer over her. I started to pray in tongues, and with my eyes closed, I saw, with my spiritual eyes, a beautiful white light around her. She had been washed clean. I encouraged her to walk with sisters in Christ and call on them to pray for her protection when she is moved to serve the Lord.

We prayed a little more for her father and sister, who were having health issues. I explained about generational curses causing problems down the bloodline of families.

The woman mentioned she attended a church and that it was people in her church that she was helping to "clear their houses" of unwanted spirits.

It reminded me of a dream I had a few months earlier where the Holy Spirit showed me walking into a church. As I walked down the aisle, I saw a woman to my right with a small child sitting in the church pew. I stopped and looked at them. The little girl stared at me, and I noticed she had a charm around her neck, I looked at the mother. I told her to remove her daughter's charm, as it was cursing her.

The woman frowned and said no; her daughter sunk down toward her mother in the pew, trying to get away from me.

In my dream, I reached for the charm necklace, pulled it off the child, and then threw it down on the aisle floor. When it hit the ground, the necklace turned into a snake and slithered out of the church.

The Lord was showing me witchcraft in the church generation today, much like the women at the health food store believed she was "clearing houses," so God is clearing His house, "the church," of witchcraft and sin.

CHAPTER 3
THE ELEVATOR RIDE

HOSEA 4:6

In this dream, I was in an elevator on the top floor of a building. When the doors opened, I saw a pastor in the distance, looking bored and just playing with a baseball, tossing it to and fro in his hands for something to do. There were about five people in the room, just a very small group. As I entered to join them, he stood up, went to the pulpit, and started an engaging speech about end times, prophecies, and spiritual warfare. Everyone was very interested, and he held their attention with enthusiasm.

Then, I was back on the elevator, and I was taken one floor down.

In this scene, as the doors opened, I saw a larger group of people studying the word of God in the Bible; they were in a classroom-type setting.

Then, I was back on the elevator, going down to the lower floor to the bottom level. When the doors opened, I couldn't move forward or get out because there were hundreds of people, all chattering among themselves and socializing. No one was listening to the pastor; it was just a big, social gathering. I was shown that this is where the majority of the people choose to stay at their level of growth in the Lord.

Never wanting to learn and mature. Christians will be divided among Christians in the last days.

A few days before this dream, I had lunch with a woman, who is a Christian but not born again in her faith.

She was positively aggressive toward me in her speech as I talked about the law and boundaries of God. As our conversation moved to the Bible, she was completely lost in the truth and her world view.

The Holy Spirit was confirming to me the lower level of the elevator in my dream, where the majority of people just use the church for social gatherings and won't move into maturity for the Kingdom on Earth.

***

HEBREWS 5:12

Instead of eating solid food, you still have to drink milk. In fact, though by now you should be teachers, you still need someone to teach you the basic truth of God's word

CHAPTER 4

THE MAN WITH CROHN'S DISEASE

The Lord is close to the broken hearted and saves those
who are crushed in spirit.

—Psalm 34:18

There was a young man called Peter who my daughter met while boarding her horse on a small farm in Virginia; he also kept his horse at the same farm. When Anne would go to the barn, she would occasionally see Peter, and sometimes they would have lunch together and chat.

One day, my daughter and I were having a cup of tea at home in the kitchen when she mentioned to me that Peter had Crohn's disease. I was saddened to hear this news. Anne said, "Mom, I explained to him about generational curses, how you are in the deliverance ministry, and how God can heal him." Anne asked Peter if he would like to be prayed over and to say the deliverance prayer to break any generational curses in his bloodline; he agreed.

We arranged to meet on a Sunday, and when he finally arrived, I was aware of how weak he was. He looked very exhausted.

Peter told us that it took all of his strength to get there. I remember the image of Peter standing against the barn wall and using it for support.

He was weak but happy and full of hope. I poured the anointing oil over the palms of my hands and took his hands. He felt the tingling energy through his body when the power of the Holy Spirit was moving, and my hands got hot. As I held Peter's hands, I could feel the Holy Spirit move through me while energy flowed through his body. Quite often, the person will feel weak and fall back as the Holy Spirit moves through them. Peter fell back and leaned against my daughter, and she had her hands on his shoulders for support.

The Holy Spirit told me to tell Peter to pick up some anointing oil and to anoint himself for forty days.

I heard from the man the very next day. He was filled with joy and excitement for the first time in a long while, and Peter was full of energy. A couple of days later, I had a surprise call from his mother; she was happy that her son was feeling well. This sweet little miracle that happened on a horse farm was one of many throughout the years. I love how God brings people into my life and allows me to minister to them in quiet places. I can honestly say that I do not know the end result of how well he became or if he was fully healed from the disease, as the family packed up and moved away to Maryland two days later, but I had often thought of Peter.

I remember his posture, leaning up against the barn wall for support because he was so weak, and how joyful he was after receiving the anointing oil with two women laying hands on him and praying in the quietness of the barn.

CHAPTER 5
HIDDEN WITCHCRAFT

*None of the wicked shall understand, but the wise
shall understand.*

—DANIEL 12:10

This is how God speaks to us if you open up your spirit to receive. One day at work, a close friend of mine came up to me, and we were casually chatting when the word witchcraft came into my head. Now I wasn't thinking about the word; it just spoke clearly into my head. As I continued my conversation with the lady, I was trying to understand why this word came into my head, as it didn't seem to fit her character.

I just quietly listened to her, and as our conversation flowed, she mentioned to me that her daughter was not acting herself and seemed to be a little agitated. We prayed together for her daughter, and I continued on with my day's work.

It's important when the Lord gives you a word that you practice waiting quietly on the word, not rushing ahead, assuming it's a gigantic problem at this point. I prayed for my friend at work and for her daughter. About two weeks later, the woman at work said that while her daughter was away with her father for the weekend, she decided to clean her daughter's room, and while she was cleaning it, she noticed under the bed that there was a Ouija board hidden away.

This is where the Lord had put the word witchcraft in my head. I told my friend at work to remove it and throw it out or burn it if it was possible, then anoint her daughter's room and speak peace over the household; everything went back to normal in her home. Now this is where life gets tricky. We walk through every day life with peace in our homes, and then suddenly you notice a change in the atmosphere. This is when you need to learn to listen to the Holy Spirit. If there is a change in the environment around you, call on the Holy Spirit to show you anything he wants you to see. Isaiah 54:17 says that no weapon fashioned against you shall prosper, and every tongue that speaks against you shall be condemned, for this is the inheritance of the servants of the Lord.

This verse is extremely powerful. When you call on this verse, you will be putting up a supernatural hedge of protection around you, your family, and the people you're praying for. This is why it's so important to know God's word in the Bible. His word is our protection here on earth. When His people speak His word, heaven and earth collide and move together. As children of the living God, we have a protective role to play here on earth as we pray for others. It is important that before we take on any assignments that the Lord has put on our hearts, we pray and ask for forgiveness for anything that has offended him whether it is a thought, deed, or action. By confessing this, we are a clean slate and able to proceed forward on our assignments unhindered by the enemy.

CHAPTER 6

THE HOUSE OF SPIRITS

MATTHEW 18:18

One night, I had a dream that I was standing on a high hilltop, the sun was shining, and I was aware of carrying a huge cross in front of me. I could see below, down in a valley, that it was dark. There was a lonely house with open windows, torn curtains, and spirits flying in and out and around the property. As I stood on that sunny hilltop, I was thinking to myself, I'm glad I'm up here in the warm sunshine and not down the valley in that dark place. Then, all of a sudden, I felt myself being propelled from my back and pushed so quickly all the way down into the dark valley and into the house that was filled with spirits.

I could see with my spiritual eyes all the demons and spirits swarming around the house until I spoke to the spirits, and they all fled.

As I stood in the middle of the house, I noticed I had anointing oil in my hand. the Holy Spirit took charge of me, and I found myself speaking in a foreign tongue—my spirit language. I quickly anointed all the walls and windows in the home, and then all the demons disappeared. A voice came into my head and said, "Do not forget the attic." I walked around the house, looking for the attic. When I found it, I climbed up and anointed the inside of the attic, throwing my oil into the space.

When I woke up that morning, the dream was still very clear in my mind, so I went to my journal, wrote everything down, and then prayed over what I had seen.

Two years later, the dream about "the house of spirits" was ready to be revealed. God prepared the work in heaven; we speak it, then manifest it on earth.

***

On that day, I will answer, says the Lord; I will answer the heavens, and they shall answer the earth (Hosea 2:21).

***

You will notice from time to time in this book that I will mention horses, as they are a big part of my life and ministry. My own beautiful horse named Victory, or Tory for short, has accompanied me on assignments for the Lord in the spiritual realm.

A horse riding friend of mine by the name of Lola was planning on going to a horse show. We took lessons from the same trainer, but I did not know Lola extremely well, only through seeing her at the shows.

I was on a website looking to see the upcoming horse shows, and I saw Lola's name entered for that weekend. I contacted her to see if anybody else was riding in her group, but she told me her trainer was out of town, so she was going on her own. I asked Lola if she would like some company and some help with her horse. Lola was happy to have my help, and we made plans to meet up. I met her at the showground that weekend; Lola had a great couple of classes and won her divisions. We were both very happy at how well she had placed; we untacked her horse and let him rest, eating hay by the horse trailer. Then we sat in the shade under a tree, drinking Gatorade and taking the opportunity to get to know each other a little better.

As our conversation flowed from horses to family and life, Lola also asked me about myself and boldly said, "I need your help with a problem" that she had at her home. She proceeded to tell me that she felt uncomfortable in her home and that there were spirits she would feel the presence of around her home and inside the house. She continued on in the conversation. The Holy Spirit quickened my spirit to the dream I had two years prior, which I called "the house of spirits." I listened carefully to everything she was sharing with me and told her I would pray about it and let her know.

I had attended a Christian conference; there, a woman spoke over me, saying that the Lord knows you are unsure sometimes of the assignments that He sends you.

The Lord said, "Don't be concerned. I will protect you; go forth and do my will. This is the house with the unclean spirits." The next day, I made arrangements with Lola to come to her home.

That evening, as I prepared to do the Lord's will, I had fasted the day before and then packed my anointing oil. As I slept that night, the Holy Spirit woke me up with the Bible verse Matthew 18:18, which says what's bound on earth is bound in heaven; what is loose on earth is loose in heaven. The Lord was showing me that something was bound in this home, and it was getting ready to be freed up. Amen.

That morning as I was preparing to meet Lola, the Holy Spirit spoke to me again and told me to bring a trash bag. I thought this was odd. However, I obeyed, folded a trash bag neatly into my purse, and drove to my destination.

Lola was happy to see me, and we chatted away about horses. Then her husband joined us as I prepared them for the deliverance. Before I do anything in the home, I like to make sure everybody that is involved is a born-again Christian. I asked them to reconfirm their faith with me, and then we prayed the sinner's prayer; I anointed them as well as myself. I began downstairs, starting in the kitchen and dining room, opening doorways, windows, and anointing any point of entry.

As I walked around the downstairs, speaking in the spirit and anointing the home, everything was peaceful in the lower part of the house as I spoke in the spirit. Then I proceeded upstairs, opening windows and anointing the space. The master bedroom was calm. There were three spare bedrooms; two of the rooms were where activity was manifesting. In one of the rooms, I opened a dresser drawer, and I found a piece of burnt sage. I took out my trash bag that the Holy Spirit had told me to bring, and I discarded the burned sage. Then I was drawn to some furniture that had been dismantled and was up against a wall. I pulled the furniture away from the wall and looked behind it.

There were two voodoo masks that had belonged to a relative who traveled to Africa, and they had been brought back innocently as a souvenir and were left in the house. Unbeknownst to the family, these artifacts carried curses that were brought into the home; these objects were added to the trash bag.

I moved down the hallway to another room, and everything was peaceful as I anointed the area. I continued into the next room, where I felt a heavy presence of activity. When the Lord had taken me in a dream a few years ago and shown me the house, I walked through the space in the spiritual realm. I could see the charged atmosphere of demons in this room as my spiritual eyes were opened.

It reminded me of squatters who were not supposed to be there. I saw three entities, two of them on a bed and one walking around, and as I stood that day with my anointing oil, all I could feel was heaviness in the room. I opened the window and anointed the beds, furniture, and doorway. As I walked out of the room, the Holy Spirit spoke in my head and told me to don't forget the attic, which quickened my spirit to remember that I was told this two years ago in a dream. I asked Lola where the attic was. We opened the hatch, and I sprinkled anointing oil over the area. I love how the Holy Spirit makes sure that nothing is forgotten that He reveals to you.

As I left the home, I remembered that Lola had once said she felt unsafe on her land, so with the remaining anointing oil, I poured it over the land and spoke a blessing on the property line. The next day, I received a text from Lola saying that, for the first time, she felt safe walking on her land in the dark. Then I began my forty days of Psalms 91 as a hedge of protection around Lola, her family, home, and property line.

CHAPTER 7
HATTERAS ISLAND

Therefore, if anyone is in Christ, he is a new creation.
The old has passed away; behold, the new has come.

—2 CORINTHIANS 5:17

This was a birthday weekend for me; my daughter had invited me to go to Hatteras Island for the weekend to celebrate and to ride horses on the beach. As we started to make preparations for the weekend away, a work colleague friend of mine mentioned that her uncle and aunt lived on Hatteras Island and that he was a pastor of the United Methodist Church.

My fun getaway weekend with my daughter on Hatteras Island was approaching, and my good friend at work asked if I would take some time while I was there to stop by and visit her aunt and uncle. She had mentioned that her uncle had been unwell and asked if I would pray with him for healing. I was honored to help, and so I made a mental note to stop by on our way out at the end of the weekend. My work friend Dvina had excitedly mentioned that her uncle flew planes and offered tour rides to tourists visiting the area, mentioning that her uncle said he would love to take me and my daughter up in the plane to sightsee.

Anyone who knows me well knows that I have a mild fear of heights, so I consciously made sure that our weekend was packed with lots of things to do so I would only visit her aunt and uncle on the way out of Hatteras Island, leaving a short time to visit them, and to avoid the trip in the air sightseeing from above.

As we went over the bridge entering the outer bank islands of North Carolina, I noticed lots of little United Methodist churches scattered throughout the drive. This seemed odd to me as I thought there would be other denominations, but nearly all I saw were United Methodist churches.

I would find out later from David that he was a descendant of John Wesley of the Methodist Church, which in 1828 on Ocracoke Island, North Carolina, was the first Methodist Church. Then a Methodist church was built on Hatteras Island; they are scattered throughout Kitty Hawk and surrounding areas.

Anne and I checked into a hotel and took our beach chairs and headed straight for the beach. We sat out there and just enjoyed listening to the waves and putting our feet in the water. We had picked up some food on the way and decided to eat outside while we were on the beach that evening.

The next day, my daughter had planned a mom-and-daughter trail ride on the beach; both being horse riders, this was the highlight of our trip. The ride on the beach was so much fun; Anne had arranged a private ride so that we would just ride together with the tour guide. The guide knew that we had experience in riding, so she allowed us to take the horses on the sand and gallop along the ocean while she watched from a distance. As we were coming back, she was taking photos of us. It really was a memorable birthday weekend.

The following morning, we visited a coffee shop for breakfast and were greeted by a friendly dog named Hattie, named after the island of Hatteras.

We spent the rest of the day kayaking, which was great fun. The canals wove through the backs of people's homes and then out to the sound; it was very scenic. As our afternoon was coming to a close, we gathered our things from the hotel and started our drive home, remembering to stop off at Dvina's aunt and uncle's house on the way out.

As we pulled into the driveway, we were greeted by a cheerfully relaxed man walking toward us dressed casually in beach clothes and flip-flops, which is typical wear for the lifestyle of living at the beach.

The man's name was David, and he and his wife Donna invited us in to their home. We sat and had some iced tea, chatting away and getting to know each other.

Then David's wife spoke with my daughter Anne and invited her to go on to the upper level of the house to see the views so that I could talk and pray with her husband, David. We prayed and shared testimonies for over three hours. When you're in an atmosphere of healing and restoration, you have no concept of time, just the sheer joy of serving the Lord.

I shared with David some of the deliverances I had experienced, that these had all been brought about through training with the Holy Spirit, and that I myself had to be delivered from some generational curses that had run down through the bloodline of my family. David was curious about generational curses as he had heard me mention witchcraft and Freemasonry several times in our conversation. David said that he was a Mason and the generations of his family were all masons and part of the United Methodist Church. He told me that they even had a

Masonic Bible in their home. I explained that sometimes when people speak of oaths, it can bring a curse into the bloodline back to the fourth generation. I anointed him, prayed for full restoration of his health as he was suffering from cancer, and asked him if he would like to say the deliverance prayer. David mentioned that he would like to talk to his wife Donna about the deliverance prayer and that they plan to say the prayer together. I told him exactly what to do as he was a minister at one of the United Methodist Church, and I trusted David to follow my instructions. I asked him to text me and let me know when he was planning on speaking the deliverance prayer with his wife and that I would be in prayer with them also.

A few months later, David and Donna were in my hometown visiting their relatives, so I had the opportunity to see them again. They were very happy for our paths to cross again; they shared with me that the very afternoon that I left the home, David and Donna went through their home and collected all items pertaining to Freemasonry. They gathered them up, even an old Masonic Bible that had been passed down through their families; they burned all items and the Masonic Bible that were connected to the occult.

David's health improved, and he enjoyed many years at his church and taking people flying.

CHAPTER 8

DUNGEONS AND DRAGONS

MATTHEW 12:43–45

The title here does not necessarily reflect the literal Dungeons & Dragons game, but it is a doorway to explain people's habits and lifestyles that can eventually destroy their environment and relationships.

A dear Christian friend of mine who lives nearby contacted me to ask if she could send a person in my path for deliverance. The man's name was Brian, and he was coming under spiritual attack in his home. When I say spiritual attack, I mean something dark that should not be there and has crossed over into the natural.

Most of the time, people live peaceful lives in their homes, but once in a while, when there are circumstances or unclean habits that are formed, doorways can be opened up in the unseen realm. And this is how it all began for Brian.

I had agreed to speak with him to discuss his situation if it was the Lord's will. My neighbor gave me his contact information, which I prayed over, and then a couple of days later I contacted the man. He lived in a different state, so his deliverance would be over the phone.

I arranged to call Brian when I was on my way to see my horse. The peaceful pastures and quietness of the barn always make me feel close to the Lord and draw on his presence.

As I approached the horse farm, I drove up the long driveway and parked my truck behind my trailer that sits in front of the barn. I pulled out Brian's phone number and opened the windows in my truck. It was a warm summer day, and I reached for my deliverance paperwork and Bible out of my purse, then dialed his number. As soon as I heard Brian's voice, I could hear his concern, fear, and worry; he was very anxious to make things right in his home.

When I'm preparing for a deliverance, it's like unraveling a mystery. I carefully map the history of the person, where they have been recently, their environment, and also who they have been in contact with or what they have been doing recently to cause the problem.

Then I put the pieces of the puzzle together, and through prayer, dreams, and confirmations, I began the work of deliverance, healing, and restoration.

The call to Brian was very businesslike; I explained to him the seriousness of a deliverance and the consequences of making light of his circumstances. As a servant to the Lord, I would know if he was lying, so I asked Brian to tell me everything truthfully from the beginning, holding back nothing—the good, bad, and the ugly—or I would not waste my time. This may sound a little harsh, but I'm very protective of the people that the Lord puts in my path as well as carefully listening to the Lord about where he wants to lead me.

Over the years, the Holy Spirit has brought a select group of chosen people into my life known as "The Warriors Gathering," fondly known as "The Gatherers." They all pray and stand by me when I need them for healing or deliverance. The Holy Spirit handpicked each individual person in the prayer group because of their loyalty and warrior hearts for the Lord.

Here is Brian's story.

Brian explained to me that he was an avid video gamer, the games he played were dark and violent, that's all he told me. As he became more and more addicted to the gaming he was aware that the atmosphere in his home changed, he would hear noises at night and have frightening dreams. Brian also explained that his three-year-old son was having nightmares and didn't want to stay in the house. I'm sure Brian must've realized at this point things were getting out of control. I reassured him that everything was going to be okay but we had some work to do and he was to follow my instructions explicitly. The first thing I did was anoint myself with oil to wash myself clean with a repentance prayer, asking the Lord to forgive me of anything that might've offended Him, so that I was a clean slate in the supernatural and could not fall under attack in enemy territory.

1 Peter 5:8: Your enemy the devil prowls around like a roaring lion looking for someone to devour.

I had emailed the deliverance papers to Brian, and before we spoke over the prayer, I asked him to reconfirm his faith in Jesus Christ and to ask the Lord to forgive him of anything that has offended our Savior. I told Brian to step outside of his home on a deck or back yard, anywhere except inside his house. We both prayed and spoke out aloud the deliverance prayer, breaking off generational curses going back to the third and fourth generation. We finished and said amen.

My protocol after speaking the deliverance is to pray Psalms 91 every day for forty days; I also have the person receiving the deliverance repeat the prayer for forty days along with me.

As I was preparing to finish up the deliverance, I talked to Brian about making some changes to his home. I asked him to go back to his home and walk through his house, opening up the windows and anointing each room, speaking the blood of Jesus. Also, to remove all of his violent video games, which were the root cause of his problems, and to play peaceful Christian music to change the atmosphere, this was to be played 24–7. I told Brian to get a small box, then go into each room of his home to look and see if there's anything that was offensive to the Lord, like a false idol, the wrong books for reading or magazines. Once he had accumulated everything that he felt was unclean, as Brian was now washed clean in the love of Christ, he was to remove those items and burn them.

Brian was allowed to contact me if he had any questions or concerns; however, the purpose of the deliverance is to help people understand that they are a new creation in Christ and Jesus is the light of the world. The light has nothing to do with the dark; now that he had been freed up from the demonic, the Lord would work in him a new heart to be able to recognize the power of light over the darkness.

I instructed Brian what to do if there was any activity at night causing him to be fearful; he was to speak with authority and plead the blood of Jesus over his home and for his son.

A week into praying Psalms 91 for Brian and his family, I received a text from him saying his son was having nightmares. The enemy always tries to attack the weakest . He followed my instructions, and everything calmed down. Brian was learning that the enemy is weak and we are strong in the Lord. He only had to learn to speak with authority and truth, knowing with confidence that the darkness would back away from the light. Finally, as we were preparing to finish the forty days of Psalms

91, I noticed a change when I spoke with him. Brian was speaking with the confidence of a Christian walking with the Lord daily. My final text from Brian was pure joy that he had peace and happiness in his home.

Most of all, his young son had noticed the change as well, saying to his dad, "You're not playing scary games and loud music anymore. I like the Jesus music that you're playing. I'm happy here."

My final words to Brian were to not fall back into bad habits, as the enemy would come back with vengeance.

It is written.

Matthew 12:43–45. When a defiling evil spirit is expelled from someone, it drifts along through the desert looking for an oasis, some unsuspecting soul to devour. When it doesn't find anyone, it says, I'll go back to my old haunt. On returning, it finds the person spotlessly clean and vacant. It then runs out and rounds up seven other spirits more evil than itself, and they will move in.

That person ends up far worse off than if he never cleaned up his home in the first place.

Although I never met this man or will hear from him again, I'm glad to know that Brian is forever changed by the experience and will be a light for others around him. Sharing his testimony is the greatest gift.

CHAPTER 9

THE SLEEPING MAN

MATTHEW 17:20

This beautiful testimony shows how the Holy Spirit teamed up with God's people here on earth.

One of the women in my prayer Gatherers group is a nurse; her name is Elaine, and she is a mighty warrior in God's world. I think of her as Deborah in the Bible. Elaine was working the night shift at her hospital one busy night, and the Holy Spirit supernaturally used the two of us for healing.

It was the middle of the week, and I had gone to bed listening to some beautiful music called Yahweh; it's instrumental, very peaceful, and relaxing.

While the music was playing, I was relaxed and reading, and then I heard the Holy Spirit say, "Send this music to Elaine." I was a little distracted when the Holy Spirit spoke, and I carried on reading my book. Again, the Holy Spirit said, "Send this music to Elaine." I sent a brief message for her to play it. I had no idea what that was all about; I just forwarded the music on to Elaine's cell phone number, continued reading my book, and eventually went to sleep.

I keep my phone charger in my kitchen, so it wasn't until I woke up and came downstairs that I saw multiple texts on my cell phone. While I slept through the night, Elaine was busy working her night shift at the hospital.

As she saw my number come through on her phone, she read my text, letting her know that the Holy Spirit had instructed her to play this music.

Elaine was having a very stressful evening. A patient was dying because he had been in a motorcycle accident. His lungs had collapsed, and his organs were failing. The patient was in a coma and on life support; his wife, who was by his side in the room, was hysterical. Elaine tried to console her, but the wife lay near her husband, crying with no hope. Elaine quietly offered to pray with the woman, but all the wife could do was lift her head up, filled with tears, and say, "Why?"

The nurse turned on the music that I had forwarded. It played quietly, permeating through the room. Elaine said to the woman, "Matthew 17:20 says because you have so little faith, truly, I tell you, if you have faith as small as a mustard seed, you can say to the mountain, move from here to there, and it will move; nothing will be impossible for you."

The room was now filled with the beautiful sound of music, and the atmosphere changed from fear to peace. The wife slowly lifted up her exhausted body and asked Elaine, "What's that music? I like it." The woman said to the nurse, "I'm ready to pray," so they prayed together for a full recovery over her husband's life.

This is when God moved in and supernaturally performed a miracle on the husband, bringing life instead of death. Elaine came back to work the next day to do her evening shift, and she saw a beautiful site. As she walked into the room where the man had laid the night before dying in a coma, he was now sitting up, fully recovered, and eating. His wife was smiling, and they had the Christian radio station playing music. What a joyful scene to behold because of his wife's faith. Even though it was only small, God moved mountains to save her husband.

CHAPTER 10

A CURSE TURNED INTO A BLESSING

No weapon that is formed against you shall prosper, and every tongue that shall rise against you in judgment shall be condemned. This is the inheritance of the servants of the Lord, and their righteousness is of me, says the Lord.

—Isaiah 54:17

A woman contacted me about her sister in England; she told me that her sister Kyla had become involved in a new age religion in California and was coming under attack. The woman believed that her sister had mixed into the occult crowd and was now being cursed by the people she was associated with.

The main person in the occult was called Michael, and he had put a curse on Kyla; her money had been stolen from her, and the curse made her bedridden and paranoid.

I had arranged to meet and talk with Kyla via Skype, as she was in England and I was in America. When we were connected online, the first thing I saw was her bound to her bed, dark eyes, very weak and fearful. Kyla was afraid to look into my eyes as she believed the enemy could look into my soul and cause harm to me. I snapped her out of that theory, assuring Kyla that no harm would befall her. Isaiah 54:17 says, "No weapon fashioned against me shall prosper, and every tongue that speaks against me shall be condemned, for this is the inheritance of the servants of the Lord."

I began the deliverance prayer, first by praising Jesus and praying in the spirit. Kyla became stronger and felt safe. I asked her to walk through her home, opening windows, and to command the enemy to leave. Kyla removed objects that had been given to her by Michael; they were placed in a bag to be destroyed or burned, as these objects had been cursing her. A lot was accomplished during our hours on Skype, but before we ended our phone conversation, I asked her to forgive Michael, who had cursed her, because the enemy cannot move in an atmosphere of love. The name Michael in the Bible means "who is like God;" St. Michael in heaven conquered Satan, so we turned the curse into a blessing and started to pray for Michael, who had cursed Kyla. The Bible verse Hosea 4:6 came to my mind: "My people perish for lack of knowledge." Michael could no longer hold power over Kyla because he was being blessed, and he could not move in an atmosphere of love. Kyla and I prayed Psalms 91 every day for forty days, and she was blessed and recovered. A couple of months after helping her, she messaged me and said that she was going back to California and wanted to pray and speak a blessing over the place where she had been cursed. I kept in touch with her during her journey, and she went to a church and was baptized. God is so loving and kind; the place that cursed her, she returned filled with the Holy Spirit and blessed that space.

CHAPTER 11
SPIRITUALLY HUNTED

There are sacrifices you make when serving the Lord, especially if you're entering enemy territory in His name. Whenever I'm preparing for deliverance and praying for the circumstances or people, I never know the severity of the situation; only the Holy Spirit knows. That's why there has to be such attention to detail, like waiting on the Lord for confirmations, and in my case, the way the Lord has trained me, which he shows me in dreams before I enter the assignment.

When I'm actively busy in the deliverance, during my forty days of praying Psalm 91, I often have dreams of being stalked by witches, warlocks, dragons, snakes, wolves, and assassins. This is because in the unseen world, you're breaking into an atmosphere where people are spiritually bound. It could be someone or a circumstance that has been bound, possibly for generations, and the enemy does not like to let go.

Matthew 18:18 tells us that what's bound on the earth is bound in heaven, and what is loose on earth is loose in heaven.

As a human being walking in our earthly flesh on the earth, there are so many things we don't understand. This Bible verse, Matthew 18:18, shows us that some of our actions in this world can cause spiritual problems in the heavenly realm, affecting our spiritual growth. Our actions and decisions play a tremendous role in our destiny; here are a few examples of things that have occurred to me during deliverances.

***

WITCHES, WARLOCKS, AND SNAKES

In my experience, as I obey the Lord in spiritual warfare, witches and warlocks are always related to addictions and witchcraft. Whenever the Lord has used me in deliverance under these circumstances, I can guarantee these enemies will show up. Their first tactic is to make me doubt my assignment, but the Holy Spirit speaks to me and says, "Go forth into the Lord's will." In dreams, witches often show up in threes, representing an unholy trinity. They always try to bind me, but I break free. They will also try to touch me; that's when I speak in my heavenly language, and they back away.

***

DRAGONS AND SNAKES

In this section, I'm going to explain about dragons and snakes. The spiritual demons always seem to appear when there is false religion, false idols, or Freemasonry.

It doesn't always have to be an assignment that the Lord has put in my path; it can be in the environment that I'm in. For example, one time we were invited to a restaurant that specialized in tapas. I was new to the deliverance ministry and still in training with the Holy Spirit. I remember we met with a group of people, and as I entered the restaurant, I became sensitive to the environment that I was entering. I had not prayed over where I was going, and I still didn't pray as I entered this restaurant; I just followed everybody else to the table. As we walked through a section of the restaurant, the paint on the walls was very dark—almost black, I would say—and then, to my right, I noticed there was a giant Buddha painting in red. I felt in my spirit that I should not be there because I was in enemy territory, but everybody that was within our group was happy to be there and try the food out. When you walk with the Lord daily, you become alien to the natural world, always consciously aware of what the Holy Spirit wants to reveal. In this particular incident, I was being shown that I was in enemy space as we began to place our orders for food. I was keenly aware that my sense of smell and taste were gone as well as my appetite.

I was woken up early in the morning with a puff of breath on my face, like a quick, firm blow to my face. As I tried to adjust my eyes to the darkness of my bedroom, I was aware that in the corner of the room, I saw something tiny in red watching me—it was a dragon. Once he knew he had my attention and that I was staring back, it supernaturally flew toward me, getting bigger in size until it covered my bed and was up to my face. I quickly spoke the blood of Jesus; it stopped in its tracks and disappeared.

I know the Lord uses many wonderful people in the deliverance ministry, and each person has their own way of walking with the Lord and serving him. So as I share my experiences, I understand and respect that there are many different approaches in the spirit realm that people use.

Snakes can be related to the occult, religious idols, and Freemasonry at all degrees. Once I was on an assignment to do a deliverance in the home of a former Masonic family. A woman was renting the home on this particular property, which had generations of Masonic family members living in it over time. As I was preparing for the deliverance and praying for a confirmation of the property, I had dreams of snakes all over the floors of this property and then a giant snake that was trying to block me from leaving the home. Fortunately, the Holy Spirit had sent an armor bearer who quickly kicked the snake and led me out of the property.

***

WOLVES AND ASSASSINS

Like some of the other circumstances I have shared, I will quite often dream of being stalked by wolves and assassins. The wolves are always following my scent and never quite catch up to me; the assassins are the same way. I remember one time in my dream, I was in this tall building, and somebody kept following me, but I was always able to turn the next corner. Then I found myself outside the building, and it was as white as snow. I woke up.

CHAPTER 12

FALSE IDOLS

Little children keep your selves from idols.

—1 JOHN 5:21

This story is an example of changes over time in nations, countries and people's beliefs. As people migrate to different countries, whether to live with families or to get away from persecution, there is always a shift in culture, beliefs, and rituals that they bring to their new dwelling.

America was once a strong Christian country; it is now increasingly being introduced to false religions and idols. This is seen in the department stores where idols of Buddha and other artifacts of people's cultures and religions are available to buy and purchase for your home. Unless you're walking with the Lord on a daily journey, it's hard to understand how little changes in your environment and atmosphere can cause a shift in your lifestyle and health. I will share with you a testimony of God's love for His people and how He answers prayers when we are desperate for an explanation.

Little children, keep yourselves from idols (1 John 5:21).

You shall have no other gods before me (Exodus 20:3).

For there is one God, and there is one mediator between God and man, the man Christ Jesus (1 Timothy 2:5).

***

I received a text from a friend whose name is Kim. It had been a while since I had spoken to her as she and her husband had moved away and bought a little farm in New Kent, Virginia.

Kim had explained to me in her text that she had been diagnosed with a rare form of breast cancer that affected her blood, and asked if I would keep her in my prayers.

I was crushed when I heard the sad news. I reminisced over all the fun trail rides we shared together on her endurance horses years before.

I went to the Lord in prayer and prayed about what I had heard; my heart ached for her circumstances. As I prayed to the Lord, He showed me why she was ill and what had caused the cancer. While in prayer, an audible voice spoke clearly into my head and said, "False idols." After hearing the voice of the Holy Spirit, I had hope and joy knowing that Kim's sudden illness was not a result of ill fate but rather something she had introduced into her life and atmosphere. This had caused her to come under physical and spiritual attack.

That night again, I asked the Lord to reveal to me the circumstances of Kim's fate and what he wanted me to do.

As I slept that night in the early hours of the morning, I had a dream that my old friend Kim and I were riding our horses in a beautiful meadow. We were talking and laughing; it was so peaceful. Then Kim walked away on her horse toward a dark wooded area. I saw a whirlwind spiral tunnel pulling objects towards it. Along the tree line where the forest was dark, I saw wolves prowling around, watching Kim approach. I rode my horse toward her and shooed the wolves away, then called out, "Kim, stay away from the darkness." She followed me back into the light of the meadow.

When I woke in the morning, I was excited that the Lord had taken me on a journey in a dream and shown me that I was to play a role in her healing.

I texted Kim that day and arranged for us to meet up so that I could anoint and pray over her; she was excited for me to come and visit her new home.

We live today in the midst of a revival of evil, so we need dreams and visions to sustain us; the promises of God are more than all the power of evil.

The book of Zechariah contains many visions and apocalyptic images; he was a visionary prophet. Even though we live in different times than Zechariah, God continues to speak to his people through dreams and visions.

Matthew 28:20 says I am with you always, even to the end of time.

No matter how many times I've been shown something in a dream I always ask the Lord for three confirmations, then I am confident that it is the Lord's will as I start to prepare for the assignment given to me.

Confirmations that I mentioned can come in different forms; sometimes a prayer warrior friend will confirm a dream that I had, or another may text me and tell me that the Lord told me to go forth and do his will, or the Holy Spirit may continue to take me to that same dream a couple of times. There is so much we don't understand about whom we are in the spirit realm, and sometimes I will delay the mission for a while just because life gets in the way and we have other obligations within our family. Then the Holy Spirit will nudge me and say, "Hurry up." I'm always aware of the seriousness of healing and deliverance, as the enemy knows who you are in God's army and what you're about to do. The enemy will taunt you in dreams and everyday life to try and deter you from your assignments. I refer back to the section on "Spiritually Hunted."

My daughter had requested to come along and see Kim, as she is an avid horse rider and had ridden many times with us on the trails with her horse.

As I prepared to visit Kim, I made a little gift basket made up of herbal teas, anointing oil, lavender, and a book of everyday prayers.

My daughter and I had a fun drive to Kim's property, and when we approached her farm, we were greeted with the familiar horses that we had once ridden, who were happily grazing in the fields.

Kim came out to greet us, and we were all so happy to reunite again. First things first, we had a tour of the farm, stables, and petting the horses, chatting away, and catching up.

Then we went up to the house; Kim led the way and showed us the inside. As I entered the family room, the first thing that struck me was the confirmation of what the Lord had shown me in a prior dream. There sat on top of the fireplace a giant Buddha statue, and then over to the right in the dining room was another idol of a Hindu god. This was the confirmation from when the Holy Spirit spoke to me about the words "false idols." After seeing the signs, I knew I was right on track with the Lord's will. I quietly thanked Him in prayer while I continued the house tour in casual conversation about our families and her health.

To Kim, this was a visit with two old friends coming to comfort her during a stressful time in her life and to lift up her spirit.

But unbeknownst to her, God was working behind the scenes to strengthen her faith in the truth. Like most of us in the Western world, we were deeply rooted in Christian faith as children, and then, as time went on, we became more influenced by worldly things and distractions, becoming more drawn to new ideas, opinions, and beliefs. This is why the Bible is so important to read because God's word is living; it speaks to your spirit.

Hebrews 10:16: I will put my law in their minds and inscribe it on their hearts; I will be their God, and they will be my people.

We continued our time together and went out to have lunch at a nearby restaurant. Then when we came back to her home before we said goodbye, I asked Kim if I could pray over her and anoint her. We all held hands and prayed, then my daughter and I headed home.

I never mentioned to Kim while I was with her about the dreams and the words that were spoken about her because, for some reason, I felt it wasn't the right time to speak to her about what I was shown, so I waited on the Lord.

The next day, I received a text from Kim saying how much fun she had the day before with us and that she appreciated the anointing and prayers. At that moment, my spirit was on fire for God. I shared with Kim what the Lord had spoken to me about false idols and the confirmation in her home, as well as the dream of us riding together and how the Lord was using me to guide her away from the darkness back into the light of Jesus.

I told Kim to reconfirm her faith in Jesus and ask for forgiveness, then remove the false idols in her home and smash them up and throw them in the trash.

A couple of days later, I received another text, and Kim said, "Lots of people said they would pray for me, but you prayed and addressed my soul. Thank you."

CHAPTER 13

MUSIC AND TEARS

PSALM 56:8

*You have taken account of my wanderings; put my
tears in your bottle, are they not in your book.*

—A WORD AND BLESSING FROM THE TRAILBLAZER

There is a beautiful piece of music called Yahweh by DappyTKeys;
it's my favorite piano music that I call on to meditate and pray
when I'm facing difficult situations.

Years ago, my dad and brother were both very ill at different
times. I would soak in that music as I prayed for their health.
Something happens to your spirit when you are soaking in music
and praying for healing. Music and weeping can call on the presence of the Holy Spirit; tears for longing are precious in God's
sight when they are tears for intercession, as well as tears of joy
for answered prayers. These are forms of prophetic intercession,
which is an open doorway from heaven to earth, so next time
someone asks you to pray for them, play peaceful music and let
the Holy Spirit take you to a secret place where your tears will
flow for the well-being of another.

CHAPTER 14

A HURRICANE AND UPHEAVAL FOR THE NATION

When the righteous are in authority, the people rejoice, but when the wicked rule the people groan.

—PROVERBS 29:2

There is a war in the spirit realm for the nation here in America. I woke up early in the morning, around 3:30 a.m. I was restless and couldn't sleep; I laid awake for a while, and then I started to pray for the president, nation, and my family. I fell back to sleep.

As I slept, the Lord took me into a dream where I was fully awake in my spirit. I found myself standing at my open front door. I looked outside and watched a hurricane wind whirl around. To my surprise, I saw a group of witches float down from the sky in the whirlwind; they landed close to my front door. The main female witch floated above the others and said, "Stop praying for the nation." She then proceeded to order a male warlock, who was standing in front of me on my doorstep, to "take her." He lunged forward to grab a hold of me, but he could not reach or touch me. There was peace and God's presence in my home. I spoke with authority and said, "Don't mess with God's people. It will not go well for you." Then I started speaking in the spirit. The warlock looked to the witch on his left side and said, "I can't cross over her threshold. I don't know what to do."

They all floated in to the whirling wind; again, the main witch looked at me and said, "We will be back."

CHAPTER 15

TRAILBLAZER AND THE STORM

Do not conform to the patterns of this world, but be transformed by the renewing of your mind. Then you will be able to test and approve what God's will is— he's good, pleasing, and perfect.

—ROMANS 12:2

To serve in God's army is a bridge between the spiritual and natural realms, living in both worlds because you have been born again in your spirit. You know when you are called because you have clear objectives that define victory. My name means victory; a woman once prophesied over me and said, "The Lord calls you his trailblazer; you are someone who paves a new and different path. You do things differently and have the courage to make things happen in a different way."

In my last testimony, I shared the dream of the witches and their threats. When I woke that morning, I remember talking to the Lord and telling him I was tired of my life being threatened. About a month later, I was sent an armor bearer.

He shall call upon me, and I will answer him: I will be with him in trouble; I will deliver and honor him (Psalm 91:15).

An armor bearer is someone brave who carries a shield, sword, and weapons. They are protectors. The person the Lord sent me is named Noble Warrior, and he is the storm that holds back the enemy during and after my assignments.

Noble Warrior is a master at his gift and shields me from threats and attacks in the spirit realm, as well as providing logistic support.

Chapter 16

A Messianic Curse

Thou shall not bow down thyself unto them, nor serve them, for I, the LORD thy God, am a jealous God, visiting the inequities of the fathers upon the children unto the third and fourth generation of them that hate me.

— Deuteronomy 5:9

This is a testimony of a rented house that had been owned by generational Freemasons.

As a seer in the Lord's Army, I'm shown things through spiritual eyes in dreams; seers have the ability to perceive the meaning of that which seems obscure to others and interpret and clarify the truth.

A woman that I had met called Anita had concerns over her rented house; she had lived there several years and always felt uncomfortable in the house. I was invited to meet with her and discuss the problems that were occurring within the home. Anita showed me around the property and inside the house. I assured Anita that I would pray about her home and contact her if it was the Lord's will for a deliverance to be performed in the home.

It's my custom to always pray and seek confirmation from fellow prayer warriors and prophetic friends. As I fasted and prayed over the situation, I had a dream one night that I was walking in Anita's home. It was infested with insects and spiders moving around in certain rooms. Then I went into the living room, and I saw the floor covered with small snakes slithering around. As I walked through the room, they partied away from me. Then as I was getting ready to leave the living room, a huge snake reared up in front of me and blocked my path. In my spirit I was thinking, how will I get out of this room blocked by this snake? When suddenly, the armor bearer that the Lord had sent me appeared by my side, The warrior kicked the snake so fast and supernaturally that it flew across the room, hit the wall, and fell to the ground.

Noble Warrior led me out of the room and followed me as I anointed the house, curiously watching as I went about the Lord's will. When I woke up that morning, it confirmed to me that the armor bearer was sent by the Lord as a protector. Sometimes we have our doubts when the Holy Spirit reveals things to us. We must always trust our gut feelings in situations, for God is our sunlight in the human spirit.

I contacted Anita and made arrangements to do the deliverance in her home. I was aware of some of the problem rooms within the house, as they had been shown to me in my dream, and I was able to address them without any concerns.

Noble Warrior had his first assignment in the supernatural and skillfully worked with me. I followed up with forty days of prayer in Psalms 91.

Anita contacted me a week later, sharing that she was enjoying peace in her home.

CHAPTER 17

WITCH ROAD

*No weapon that is formed against you shall prosper;
and every tongue that shall rise against you in judgment shall be condemned. This is the inheritance of
the servants of the Lord, and their righteousness is of
me, says the Lord.*

—Isaiah 54:17

It is such a marvelous opportunity to serve the living God; I
never know what amazing adventures or assignments are on the
way. Sometimes they come in the form of a person contacting
me; other times the Holy Spirit will speak a word in my head for
me to pray about and trust him. Then, other times, he will take
my spirit into a dream and show me the next assignment.

On one particular occasion, in the early hours of the morning, I dreamed of a street, and in the spirit, I was high in the sky,
looking down on a street in a neighborhood. I was shown the
street name, which read Witch Road As I watched safely above,
I observed a witch in a house on that street. She smashed several
potions, and a white smoke rose up into the atmosphere, and the
witch blew the potion down the street. A white smoke floated
down the road over every house, putting a curse on the homes.

Then the Holy Spirit showed me the street sign again, but it had a different name; it was called by its city name instead of Witch Road I felt in my spirit that, I was being shown these two names for a reason, the first one Witch Road, was to show me that a witch lived on that street and was cursing the homes.

The true name was revealed to me, so I could identify its area, When I woke up I went to work and started investigating the location, then praying and fasting for more revelation.

When you are a servant of the Lord, you must stand strong in faith and trust; they form a good perspective on life, especially when you are entering unknown territory. I called on a couple of my friends for confirmation and notified the Prayer Gatherers, who are my faithful prayer group, informing them of the next deliverance.

When Jesus died on the cross, he said, "It is finished!" Our Lord and Savior, Jesus Christ, won the victory over evil, and as we walk on this earth and serve him, it is our job to enforce the victory through our everyday lifestyle as prayer warriors. Praying is so powerful; it is where heaven and earth collide.

This was a new area of deliverance for me, covering the whole street in a neighborhood and their homes, as well as the lives of the people in those houses. I contacted my friend Jeanette who is part of the Prayer Gatherers. I discussed with her my plan for the deliverance and asked whether she would like to be a part of the journey. Jeanette was excited to serve our Lord, so we made arrangements to meet up.

It was a beautiful autumn day in October; the sun was shining and the air was cool—perfect walking weather. Jeanette and I drove over to our destination and excitedly got to work. We both had our anointing oil, our Bibles, and ours prayers ready to be released over every home on that street. We decided to alternate with each house; Jeanette would say a prayer over the homes, families, and property lines. Then I would follow with the next home. We spoke prayers from our heart, consciously watching the condition of the house and how it was kept. Then the witch's house was in sight; the home was setback, covered with bushes and trees and overgrown, in fact you'd hardly know there was a home there due to its unkempt nature. There was a cat watching us on the porch. It jumped down and came out to greet us; like most cats, it sweetly rubbed up against my leg. I leaned down, and with my anointing oil, anointed the cat's head while speaking a blessing over the property for the witch inside the house and her property line. I poured more anointing oil into the palm of my hand and sprinkled it over the garden; this was to insure everywhere was blessed.

Jeanette and I continued on to the next home, speaking a blessing and anointing the area. We now had a little visitor accompany us on our journey, and the witch's cat followed us along two or three houses down; then the cat turned around and went home. It took a couple of hours to finish up both sides of the street, then we came to the last house, and we sang and prayed over the home together; our assignment was finished. Exhausted and excited over what we had just completed, we got into my car and headed out for a well-deserved lunch.

Toward the end of the forty days of praying Psalms 91, I came under a spiritual attack. In a dream, I was being hunted down by the enemy; they had the appearance of men, and there were at least three of them. Although they looked human, their behavior was like that of an animal. In the dream, I would occasionally glance over my shoulder, and I remember running into a room and realizing there was no way out. To my shock, the men were at the door by the room. All of a sudden, the armor bearer that God had sent to me appeared. Noble Warrior stood as a guard, shielding me from the enemy. The armor that he wore was a hedge all around the two of us, and I was hidden. The beings that came in the room had animal-like instincts; they sniffed the air as if to try and find my scent, tearing draws open and moving furniture to see if I was hiding. I stood quietly, worried they could see me, but God had put a hedge of protection around my space; I was completely invisible to the enemy. Then I woke up from my dream.

When you serve a mighty God, you will experience some pain, fear, and even doubt sometimes, but God will send His chosen warrior to protect and find you, pulling you out of danger as you go forth and do His will.

CHAPTER 18

THE PSYCHIC READER

*Behold, I give you power to tread on serpents and
scorpions and over all the power of the enemy, and
nothing shall by any means hurt you.*

—LUKE 10:19

God's love is so great for his people that even when we go astray
and think we're in the right, he gently corrects us and turns everything around on the right course.

There had been a prayer request for a woman called Angela
through the Prayer Gatherers. My friend Teresa had asked me to
speak with a woman called Angela; she was seventy-seven years
old and a Christian. When I spoke with her over the phone,
she told me she was depressed, suffered from anxiety, and had
suicidal thoughts. Angela mentioned to me that many years ago
she used to do "readings" and was a psychic but doesn't practice
anymore. She mentioned that she couldn't sleep at night and
would wake up with bad dreams, seeing snakes in her room and
a big snake head at the end of her bed.

I prayed for confirmation on this assignment, and that night
I dreamed of being with Angela and doing the deliverance at
her home. In my spirit, I saw Noble Warrior outside watching

and keeping guard over the property line and atmosphere where Angela lived. When I woke up, I felt safe and was confirmed by the Holy Spirit that my assignment was on time and according to God's will.

I arranged to meet Angela for the deliverance, and the first thing that struck me about her appearance was how crippled she was—bent over, and her hands were all twisted. She could hardly walk as she met me at the door.

We sat down and had a cup of tea. She told me about her life and that she had once been a history teacher. This sparked my interest, as I have a great love for history also. Angela was fascinated with how the Lord used me in the deliverance ministry, and I shared some of my testimonies with her. The woman was still confused as to why she was being tormented with fearful dreams; she also told me that she was regularly seeing three psychics to look into her future.

I asked Angela to reconfirm her faith in Jesus Christ, and I anointed her. I said you will need to repent from practicing witchcraft as well as ask forgiveness from the Lord for the people's lives that you spoke about in the psychic readings in the past. God was waking up Angela's spirit to get right with him, closing the doors to her past.

The forty days and Psalms 91 went peacefully by until the very last day; I cannot explain this because many things with God are a mystery. I had a bizarre dream where I was in the spirit of a training room. I don't know how many lives Angela had done psychic readings over, but suddenly I had an onslaught of individual people trying to attack me. As each person entered looking normal, they immediately transformed into whatever they had medaled within the earthly world. The first was a black man; he was very dark, like a person from Africa. He blew a dart at me, but I diverted it with my arm. Then he lunged towards me, but he could not touch me. The words witchcraft and voodoo came to my mind. I never stopped speaking in the spirit until he became weak, and then I spoke the blood of Jesus over him. The man transformed into complete peace, and the demons left. Many more came into the room to be freed up, and each time I spoke in the spirit, the battle began. The last one was exhausting; it was extremely tall, pale, and large and looked like a zombie. It took many layers of demons to leave him; he kept lunging toward me and changing into different entities until they were set free. Finally, everything evaporated, and then the man turned into a normal person. He looked overjoyed and left the room. I remember in the dream feeling really exhausted and asking the Holy Spirit if I could wake up. I woke up at 4:00 a.m. I prayed and drifted back off to sleep.

Angela and I kept in touch for several weeks after her deliverance; she was sleeping so much better now and enjoying peace in her home. Little did I know that this once-history teacher would help guide me with information on the surrounding areas in which we lived that would help educate me for a future deliverance.

CHAPTER 19

THE THREE AMIGAS

*Trust in the Lord with all your heart, and lean not
into your own understanding.*

—PROVERB 3:5

This Bible verse instructs us to trust God and not our own knowledge.

I was in an office building one day when a stranger asked me, "Who are you?" I shook her hand and introduced myself. As I took her hand and smiled at her, she replied, "Are you in the body of Christ? Because I see the anointing all over you." I shared with the young woman the work of the Lord in the deliverance ministry; she asked if I would help her.

We exchanged phone numbers, and I said that I would get back to her after praying over the situation.

There were three Mexican women sharing an apartment together who all shared strong spiritual beliefs. However, something in the atmosphere was causing animosity in the apartment; there was tension and unease between the three women.

As I prayed over the situation, I received a friendly text from a close friend of mine, Betsy. She mentioned the Lord had put some words on her heart to share with me. They were encouraging words, so I made arrangements to visit the women in their apartment and help them move forward through their difficulties.

When I arrived, I was warmly greeted by Julia, Roberta, and Hillary; we sat around the kitchen table, all drinking tea and enjoying cookies. As I introduced myself, it gave me the opportunity to observe the women and confer with the notes I had written down about the characters of these three women and what the Lord had revealed to me days before.

Now, as I'm writing this book on testimonies, you should know that all the names written are different from the original people. Each person and name is very special to me. Before I ever meet them, I look up the meaning of their name. I prayed over that name and called out for their highest blessing. The first woman who had contacted me was named Roberta, and she confided in me that she had a fear of death and had even thought of suicide. The next woman was Julia, and she suffered from mental illness; something had traumatized her at some point in her life; she was unable to work and spent most of her time in her bedroom. The third woman was Hillary. I felt in my spirit that she was very resentful of something, and as I got to know her, I found out that she had been abandoned by her husband and was bitter for her difficult life ahead. She had joined the Jehovah's Witnesses to find peace but still continued to be angry about her past.

As we sat around the table, I anointed, prayed, and spoke the deliverance over each woman, addressing their specific needs and speaking a blessing over their future. I asked Hillary, who was a Jehovah's Witness, to repent for walking away from the living God and truth, then ask Jesus into her heart and reconfirm her faith. Also I was speaking peace over her fragmented heart, replacing resentment with love. In the name of Jesus Christ, I broke off the spirit of fear and death from Roberta, and then I prayed freedom from mental illness over Julia. I opened the windows in the apartment and anointed each room so that anything that was not of the Lord had to leave in Jesus' name. Hillary gathered up her Jehovah's Witness books and put them in a trash bag to be disposed of and to be removed from of the house.

When I went home, I was exhausted, and I honestly slept for two days. It can be very exhausting work but immensely rewarding. Like I always do, the beautiful prayer Psalm 91 was spoken for forty days to bless the three amigas.

CHAPTER 20

200 YEARS OF WAITING

*Do not say, I will repay evil; wait for the Lord,
and he will deliver you.*

—PROVERBS 20:22

In the early hours of the morning, I had a dream. I was on the property where my horse trainer had scheduled a lesson for me. The whole property was loud, with a whirling, strong wind sound. It was deafening and distracting. I spoke to the wind and commanded it to be at peace, in Jesus name. The wind calmed down, and all was peaceful on the property. I saw a woman in the barn; she was staring at me. I felt in my spirit that she was hungry for knowledge and truth. She had big brown eyes and dark, short hair. The woman asks me curiously, "Who are you?" Her spirit spoke to mine. There is deliverance getting ready for the Lord on this property and the people. I saw with my spiritual eyes Noble Warrior loading my horse in the trailer and putting my tack away; the armor bearer is always nearby, watching and protecting.

I will pray about the dream.

Something in this earthly atmosphere is changing; God is speaking to His prophets and seers to free up what has been stolen by the enemy. I once had a dream that the enemy had to give back everything that was stolen from God's people.

Throughout the ongoing months, I have had dreams of witches trying to follow and attack me as I continue to pray for the land. They know I will claim that land back to God.

Months later, I dreamed of a crime scene on the property that God was preparing for deliverance. I was shown three black men who were extremely fit and lean; it reminded me of a different time period a couple of hundred years ago. In the dream, two men stood side-by-side, while the third man was slightly to the side facing them. One of the two men standing together had a half-moon-shaped knife, which I researched and found out is called a sickle or scythe. The man swung the knife in the air and slit the third man through his stomach, ripping his intestines out; he fell forward in a pool of blood. I was standing in the spirit next to the man that was slain. I could see the face of the black man who was watching the murder, and there was deception in his eyes. I felt in my spirit that the man who had been slain had been lured by the men; he was completely unaware of what was going to happen.

I did some spiritual mapping to investigate the history of the land. As I continued my research, I would come under attack again through dreams, with witches stalking and threatening me, trying to pull me away from my goal for God's kingdom.

***

THE YEAR 1853
Through courthouse records and investigating the history of the farm, I found that the property was once called a different

name in the year 1853. The owner of the farm passed it down through his descendants all the way through 1911. Through courthouse records, the land had been subdivided and sold numerous times to people. One particular person who acquired a parcel of land was a man in the Navy; he had recorded in the County Courthouse of 1853 that his Negro slave was granted his freedom and given a small inheritance.

A murder was committed in the year of 1853 on the original farm; the blood that was spilled on the land has been crying out for justice for nearly two hundred years. God is faithful; there will be healing, a reclaiming of the land back to God, releasing the goodness of God upon the property and its people.

I arranged to meet with the owner, Annie, and we prayed together. She was excited for me to bless her land. I threw salt on the land, praying out loud a repentance prayer, pulling down strongholds, loosing the angels of warfare, and reclaiming the land back to God.

2 Kings 2:20–21: Never again shall this land cause death and be unproductive.

Then I sprinkled water into the atmosphere and on the earth to represent the Holy Spirit's presence and the power poured out by Jesus' followers.

The debt was canceled, and there was a release of goodness from God over the land and its people—past, present, and future.

The Holy Spirit graciously showed me, after the deliverance, the sun shining as I walked among the horses in a field; there was new life and beginnings for Annie's farm. Matthew 18:18 says what's bound on earth is bound in heaven, and what is loose on earth is loose in heaven.

Victory in His name,
The Trailblazer

CHAPTER 21

TIME TRAVEL

For God is my king from of old,
working salvation of the earth.

—PSALM 74:12

This is a message for our generation: I was taken in a dream and time traveled in the 1940s.

I found myself in the spirit and fully alert in an old-fashioned grocery store; it reminded me of something in a 1940s movie during the Second World War. I could see everything in color—the tins of coffee, flour sacks, and other articles for sale. I remember seeing the vibrant colors of red and green. I saw people neatly dressed as was fitting for that time period—coming in and out of the store, picking up supplies. As I stood there watching, I was consciously aware I was different—the clothes I wore were not from their time. Although I cannot recall what I was wearing, I knew I was not part of their world. As these thoughts were running through my mind, I sensed somebody standing behind me. I looked over my shoulder and was pleasantly surprised to see Noble Warrior on the scene. I was pleased to see him, and I spoke telepathically to him, "Can you believe we are here? Do you think they can see us?" As I continued to watch the comings and goings in the store, I looked outside and saw a busy street, old fashion cars going by, and people walking around. I knew in my spirit that this was during the time of World War II; some of the people were in war uniforms. As I continued to watch the scene outside, I thought to myself. I wanted to walk out on that street among the people, but then a little bit of self-doubt came into my mind. I wasn't sure if I should leave the safety of the old shop. As if reading my mind, Noble Warrior took my arm, linked it into his, and said, "Come on. Let's explore outside," so out the door we went. The street was bustling with life, smells, and people. They didn't seem to mind our attire; they just nodded as we walked by. A little way down the road, I saw a man repairing an old-fashioned war vehicle; the hood was up, and he appeared to be working on it. As I approached him, he turned around. and I eagerly said hello to him. He straightened up from his work and said hello. He said something very profound that resonated in my spirit: "Tell the people to prepare. A war is coming." When the man said these words, I felt he was not talking about his time zone during World War II but about my time period and to prepare for the beginning of World War III.

When I woke up, I was excited about my experience and traveling back in time. I wrote everything down in my journal, and I asked the Lord for confirmation on what I had seen in my dream.

That morning, I had some shopping to do and went to my local grocery store. As I was checking out my groceries, I chatted with the woman at the checkout, ministering to her about starting to prepare for changes and the coming war. A military man stood behind me in line and overheard my conversation. He boldly said, "She's right, a war is coming."

A WORD OF ENCOURAGEMENT
FOR THE CHANGING TIMES

If you have been chosen to read this book, my prayer for you is to find a personal relationship with the living God, and enjoy the adventures He has in store for you.

> *Proverbs 3:5–6: Trust in the Lord with all your heart, and lean not into your own understanding. In all your ways, acknowledge him, and he will make straight your paths.*